Mayssa is a poet, a feminist, a writer, a reader, and a great listener. She has a passion for teaching and building strong communication with her students. She worked as an English head of department and an English teacher for more than 15 years in various schools.

She was known as a quiet and a reticent woman among her friends and family. She believes that the less you have around, the more you gain inside.

After marriage, she decided to pursue her dream and be a published writer and had the courage to collect all her teenage prose and diary in the book The Soft Power, named by her husband who referred it to all hardworking women nowadays.

The woman in this book may seem languishing but it is by far the most realistic yet dreamy woman we can encounter in our days. She was a simple girl who lived her life anticipating tomorrow and waiting for a chance to change and thought that life was about a man until she realized that the life, she needed was about more than just a lift.

She believed that the reality of who we have become hits us hard every day to the core and makes us realize that we spend our lives living in a body that doesn't represent the soul inside us.

In this book she discusses two versions of the same woman: the simple and the evolved one. She describes her raw feelings based on her daily experiences with people who departed her life harshly and people who departed hers smoothly and people who still she learns from.

To my grandma who showed me what a great woman is.

This book is dedicated to all the women out there who are facing troubles and obstacles in their daily life to prove or show or live the way they truly are and want to.

This book is dedicated to my husband who was once the main reason for me to change from who I was before him, who was the main door to a new life that proved me wrong in all levels.

Again. To my husband who named this book and always called women "the soft power".

Mayssa Khaznadar

THE SOFT POWER

AUSTIN MACAULEY PUBLISHERS™
LONDON • CAMBRIDGE • NEW YORK • SHARJAH

ISBN – 9789948770169 – (Paperback)
ISBN – 9789948770176 – (E-Book)

Application Number: MC-10-01-0097888
Age Classification: E

Printer Name: iPrint Global Ltd
Printer Address: Witchford, England

First Published 2023
AUSTIN MACAULEY PUBLISHERS FZE
Sharjah Publishing City
P.O Box [519201]
Sharjah, UAE
www.austinmacauley.ae
+971 655 95 202

My thanks to my mother who sought liberty all her life but never found it.

To the man who made me the woman I am today.

To my children, Joseph and Giselle, who were the true joy in my life.

To my friend who held my hand and lifted my soul every time I was down.

Prologue

The woman in this book was once a strong woman until she lost herself in the roads of life. She was once a queen on her throne, and a girl that belongs to someone. Now all she feels is a different version of who she really wanted to be.

She is ready to heal herself for the sake of others. To fake a smile and show the world a happy human being.

No one knew what was going on inside and the fact is, nobody cares but to see the outside the way they wanted and are usedto.

Until the day when she opened a door deep inside and started asking questions.

Most of which had no answers… but the pain she was holding in her chest made her wake up to the ugly truth.

The truth is that she was surrounded by many, but no one was close enough to see.

No one was close enough to feel.

A Man

To a man…
whom I call my man…

When there are a lot of things insidemaybe just born
maybe found since long but closed, imprisoned in a cold room
far beyond the heart.

And now, they are smelling freedom, tasting sweet feelings,
feeling life and for the first time waiting and walking on its
path with that lovely passion to reach.

For the first time ever,
everything is new but old in a different way as if all were just
waiting for a touch to set free.

I still remember the first time I saw your face and that
trembling look between us. It was a stolen moment from our
happy life…
I still remember the first time we talked and how you said my
name.
I used to say that the start always scares me.

But talking about our real start was different.
It was something that began before it really started. When we said our first words,
it felt like a bird flying on a different land discovering everything…
trying to find the best place to build its everlasting nest.
Flying over every treeevery small place every corner.

It's a nice feeling to take things or everything alive,
that has a life maybe lived and passed or maybe is reborn with every sunrise.

I was smelling you,
I was seeing you next to me,but you weren't even there.
Your presence was there in your absence. You were hunting me down every minute…
capturing me and torturing me with loads of questions.

My man.
You may look simple but going inside you is too hard, you have many doors to be opened.

I kept myself safe and my doors hidden for so long, waiting for a real man who's going to be able to open, enter without even asking,
just without permission.

The sun was touching my face,making me see nothing but your face.

I went far with my thoughts and imagined you sitting next to me and we felt special among people, watching the sunrise. Feeling the beginning.

I really felt like talking to you or looking inside your eyes trying to find anything that helps me answer many questions and fill empty blanks.

I keep remembering your smiles…that look in your eyes.
I keep thinking of you but not like any other.
I still want to build and draw you inside me far beyond what a guy is to a girl.

I want to choose the colors to paint you. The positions I need you in
The places where you'll live inside.

I aim to feel you, my man, inside my blood and be your eyes…
share your breath to taste your life.
I aim to mingle with you so that we'll be, for real, one. All this would never be related to a simple word we say.
It's just the main door for a huge place filled with sweet houses, streets, doors, and ways.
A main door for our life together.

I keep asking questions with different tastes.
Sometimes direct; sometimes, hidden and sometimes, I ask things I don't even know how to choose the words for.

I can't stop myself from drawing your image inside me. But still, something's lost!

And my man is still far physically, but somehow close in a different way.
Just like the sweetness of winter
when you feel it inside and deeply inside but it's still far and all you do is watch
seeing it from far away.

God!
A song from Jay Sean "Ride it" keeps haunting my mind.

Is it time? Or time has another way to give me my own answers.
Sometimes, I feel it passing slowly as if it's judging me, holding days on a side and hours on a side. Staring at my body and my eyes with that cold look.
Trying to tell me many things, to make me understand what it's all about.

I'm still standing silent, carrying many things inside; some are answers which are few and most are questions that need to be answered.

My man…
I can't deny the complete image of that sweet human inside you.
Nothing is perfect as they say and as I believe, but as for an image to feel…
Sometimes, it is!

A feeling may be high, and its highness is its own way toward being perfect.
Just a true, pure, perfect feeling.

I was always able to talk with myself about my deep feelings and it's true that sometimes, I get lost in finding the right words but as for now it's totally different.
It's not that I can't find the words to express, but it's like I can't find the whole image to express.
I'm keeping it inside maybe because of its highness and maybe because I need it inside, to teach it how to get out by itself.

My man!
God! How nice it is to say out loud.
I waited so long to say, 'my man,' and I would never accept to release this word from my deepest places if I wasn't really feeling it.

But still far! Far like the magic of autumn and high as its ability to blend different colors… all together.
And close like a bird with opened wings flying over my head all the time.

My man…
my everlasting true love…my whole image.

I just aim to paint you my own and paint myself your breath
to feel life from inside you
and give it to you as perfect as autumn is.

A Silent Point

Moments in a day is all we need now.
Everything seems to be running from all around and we're standing, unable to move.

Feels weird for us to be imprisoned even for a moment without moving… without releasing our thoughts all over our body without hearing the beats of our heart.

For all our life, we've treated ourselves unfairly.
Tried to put us in the corner, far from anyone and anything.
We tried hard to squeeze our feelings inside…
to push our thoughts, our fears, our emotions, our whole soul down so nobody could really touch us.

Now we woke up realizing what we've done all these years.
And praying for a moment from God to be ours.
To set ourselves free with no bounds and no fear.

Today, we woke up to the reality of carelessness.
The reality of us being stupid of not knowing what a woman is…
and what a woman should be.

We suddenly realize that all these years, we have been building and building and building a huge castle with no windows or doors.
We ended up imprisoned with all our precious thoughts and feelings.

Unable to see what's outside or let anyone see what's inside.
I know that people look from far away or even closely and they like the view
and wish they had that castle as their own, so they can still add colors to it.

But they couldn't have even one chance to get inside and discover it though a few tried for years to find the door for this gray, mysterious, and huge castle, but are still failing till today.

It's weird how we treat our bodies, so different from our souls. As if we live in fear all the time that we can lose or maybe turn our souls angry against us.
We see us running all the time after something and facing everything and everyone that may hurt us, and we hurt others forgetting that they have a soul as well.

It's weird for us how we've never looked at our body in a good way. We cared less about it and focused a lot on our soul.

Forgetting that the mirror of the soul is the body!
Now we're paying a lot to our soul to fix that tired body.

To give beauty to it again, the one we stole from for a long time.

"How hard is life."
We hear this sentence all the time from many people.

It's just us and what we believe.
Life is a journey. We go through it and face a lot of different destinations, different ways, and different people.

It's just us not facing it the right way.
We think life is what we wish it to be…
what we dream about… what we expect mainly.

But it's reality…
all about facts and pure reality.
We keep on living and going on to what we call our life.
Then, we are shocked by a huge wall with a big screen displaying things that never came to our minds.
Things about us…
about our days… how will we be, live, love, eat, walk, and think.

Suddenly, we stand unable to even blink and start to ask questions; those with answers and those that never will have any.

In happiness, in sadness, in love, in work, in life, and in everything, there's always a BUT.

It always comes in the middle of our breath…

in every smile, in every tear, and in every moment, we live in a day.
Life was never perfect.It wasn't made perfect.

And those who think it is and it can be…
are the only ones who will face despair and ultimate sadness.
We keep wondering why God created obstacles. Why nothing is simple?
Why everything is not perfect?

Humans must think that God won't waste simplicity on possibility. Everything must have a taste if not by our senses,then by our hearts. Some things must touch us… must touch the strength melody we have inside.
How can we stand against the wind?
How can we travel in the opposite way of life?
How can we stand in the middle of the way and raise both hands with a No? Or should be considered as going against life and its rules?

For me, moments,
just moments, is all I need now.

As I feel far from my life,
far from everyone and everything. I won't say far from love as love is the breath I take every time I look in your eyes.
You can't imagine what I see from within your eyes, they are my window to life.

I see joy, hope, and faith.
I see happiness in all its colors.I see love in all its meanings.

I see me laughing and running and sometimes flying.

I see me complete with nothing but perfection in mind… peace in soul.

A Smile

How nice to begin a day with smiling as a smile is like magic nowadays,

and we rarely see it pure and coming straight from the heart. How can we reach that?

I keep asking myself all the time as if it's something impossible,

but in fact, it is, and we can't even understand how we can keep it on our lips.

Once an old man told me a smile is a cure to any disease…

For me, it's a pretend-to-be thing these days as no one is truly happy in this life.

Days keep on running and racing each other… who will be the last to end the month?

Moments keep on passing in our minds and disappear in a blink.

We don't own time, time owns us; he is the master of every day.

The king of all hours… the ultimate power in this world.

A Start

A start to
falling in love…

I woke up this morning after a very long nightwhere I slept
in the arms of my tears.
They were hugging me tight and didn't leave me till my whole
body was far away from my soul
just staying still in bed.

I woke up feeling many things but unable to understand a
thing of what's inside me.
How can I talk about something high, so painful, so
mysterious, and so confusing?

How can I just speak a word…
and words seem to be held in a place far inside me.
I tried many times to reach there but nothing was helping me
I was there all alone by myself.
For the first time, I can't know where I am…

Can my man ever be the music of my life…?
Just the music that blends and mingles with my organs and
cells,

move in my veins and blood. Would that ever be true?

Why do I seem like losing such images in my soul?
I kept dreaming and believing such things forever, but why
am I feeling it so far now?
Is this what they call love attacking me?

About Lebanon

For the first time in a couple of years, I'm here alone.
I'm here alone to feel alone and to taste those kinds of feelings that I forgot I still have inside.
I'm here all by self with the rain.
I'm here all alone to connect with my inner self once again.
I'm here to know me better.
I'm here to be here with all my senses.
There's something about this place that my soul won't get over.
A lot of memories and distances connected here.
I can hear the walls speak sometimes… words of wisdom, full of sense,
words that can transport me several years back.
Words that witnessed moments that even time won't be able to erase.
Words that hide stories of forgotten love…
Stories we read about in some old books or saw in an old movie.
I'm here to create distance so I can be able to connect again, to feel far so I can be close again.
I'm here to be able to ask maybe for a cure, forgiveness or even courage to let go.

Something I'm trying to do for a very long time but still unable to figure out how.

We think we are strong but, on the way, to connect to the inner soul we lose our way and stumble with all those memories and moments that can summarize the core of our life.

To forget, we need to face.

To hate, we need to admit and feel the love inside.

To free ourselves in the present, we need to live the past. To be able to live the future, we need to die at some stage.

Always in the Middle

In the middle of the night, you are my light.

In the middle of the day, you are the shadow I need. In the middle of the crowd, you are the silence I crave.I remember I saw your face last night…

Your body was dancing and moving on the beats of joy.For a moment, I felt your heart.

I felt you and was touched by joy.

For a moment, I felt a small girl hiding in the days and waiting for her man to grab her from arms and take her away.

For a moment, I felt so in love… A twig so attached to the tree.

A cloud so attached to the sky. A light so attached to the candle.A soft leaf.

****

I am here again as if sent back to life again or re-born after being dead for some time.

I don't know how to communicate with the new me now… All around has changed or has fallen apart, or damaged, or even passed away.

Life changed to something I don't get most of the time. Life was my friend and I used to know her…

Life was something I look for and I want, Life was me and I was in life…

And now, I stand confused, lost, and overwhelmed. A stranger here and there.

A stranger in this life and a stranger to myself.

I don't recognize the changes and I can't recognize the "me" now.

Everything seems either white or black and nothing is clear, and I have nothing in my hands to recolor it with.

As Real as This Will Sound

As real as this will sound, I never wrote to anyone who really exists in this world but my man.

But to me inside, only to find you there, mingling with my thoughts and creating a place for you.

To consider you as a man next to me,
you were never my type, but to look beyond what is there for everyone.
You are exactly the type of man found on my papers.

Tough yet emotional… Strong yet tender… Limited yet generous…
Looks like a door but you're the house itself…
Sometimes, I run out of words to describe the feeling I experience around you.

I learned the hard way that what appears for everyone in any place tells me nothing about what lies on the inside.
A world of fantasy and runaway stories of men from old ancient books. Where men were meant to be men…

as great and high as the word suggests. A world of perfect meaning of different sexes.

I learned the hard way that what is inside is only for the self, deeply concealed and unrevealed, with many burdens and obstacles appearing with its true face.

You are one of those men,

those men who exist only in books and stories, those men who rarely exist nowadays.

In the end, we try to find someone who acts the same way he feels or what truly he is.

Bodies

Bodies and Souls…

How can we live without souls?

How can we survive with a tired body and feel free?

If our souls are imprisoned in a place far away from this world?

How can we feel our senses if our souls and bodies are in war forever?

How can we taste life and its sweetness if we've lost the way?

For many years, I've tried hard to answer these and many other questions, to find the way and to taste peace.

I have tried even harder to understand the life I am in…But I always find myself standing in the same place.

Maybe, I can ask but never have answers… I tried to relate my body to its soul,

but they seem to always go for the extreme. Each in his own way,

each in his own world.

I tried to sit with both separately,

talk deeply to and put in a one bed wishing for some affair,

but they seem only attracted in bed.

They seem like a man and a woman…

attracted only for a limited time, each fulfilling his needsand in the end, turning their backs to each other…

A body is no less important than a soul.

In fact, it's the other half that completes the life of a soul.

It took me time to understand it but now eventually, it turned to be hard to digest.

They just don't understand each other, scattered, and lost in each's own world.

Bodies…

If men and women could understand the real image and use of their bodies, they will end up happy and satisfied.

Bodies are nothing but a means or a way to show the real us and the hidden unspoken words and acts inside us…

We look around and judge people by how they look and how they dress…

and how they move and act and breathe sometimes… We believe that it's what we see

and it is what they are really…It's not our fault in this.

Who is covered is called a retard and who is outgoing is called a bitch.

Who wears dark colors and who wears bright ones are under the lens?

Who talks loudly and never quiet is bossy and will never get married?

Who is quiet, is weak and will end up a housewife and a follower.

When are we going to learn that the outside has a lot to do with the inside?

Maybe it's by choice to deliver a different message or by force...
Bodies are the unspoken language of souls.
The silent touch of love to the outside... the gates to that world inside us.
It's the only way that takes us inand out...
When making love,
our bodies dance on the music of our hearts,with our soul in harmony,
completing each other.
Until then the perfect use and image is found.

Broken

Like a yellow leaf scattered all around the tree like a broken-
winged bird dying to fly
like me and like you
like any other deserted house or body
like a tree in the middle of the storm and like any other
different feeling left inside.

Like a lonely soul in the middle of the crowd and like the
noise in the middle of the silence.
Just like you and me…

Choices

I always used to say to be imprisoned in love is freedom itself,
and to be free in life is prison itself.

To be always happy in life is like being deeply sad, and to be
yourself in this life
is something far to reach.

I learned that when you laugh,
the whole world will laugh with you, but when you are in
pain,
you just cry alone.

Oh God…
People are just living at the surface.
They are like statues moved by everything except humanity.

As for me,
I learned so many things in this huge, small life.
I learned that everything we see great in life, in fact, started
by a simple idea and small beginning.
Simplicity is a treasure…
It's a great treasure that leads to everlasting happiness.
But who cares!

From this, I also learned that when I can't express what I really feel,
which is so painful, I practice feeling what I can express,
which is even harder and simpler at the same time…?
And I know none of them is equal.
But I guess that's why human beings among all mammals CRY…

Although crying is so deep, and each tear drop comes from a deep red wound,
but still, it's the simplest way we use to express without even saying a word.

There's a piece of art which I adore from Giovanni, by the name of *Choices*…
If I can't do what I want to do,
then my job is to not do what I don't want to do. It's not the same but the best I can do.
If I can't have what I want,
then my job is to want what I've got
and be satisfied that at least there's something more to want.

Since I can't go where I need to go, then I must go where the signs point
though always understanding parallel movement isn't literal.
Choices…
Sometimes, we don't have the choice to choose, or even choices won't exist,

but I believe that when we have no chance at getting what we want,
we probably won't get it.
But if we believe in ourselves,
we may probably sooner or later get it.

I always say that anyone can be special and unique in his own way.
To feel
is something we can't even control in us.
To be we always and everywhere is something really hard.
Feel like always in the middle of a crowd,
so many to see, feel, and so many to know and run from.
Life is so strange; it pushes us to change to suit the dress it puts on us.

A human being itself is a huge world. With all his feelings and things heard.He is a great lonely mystery,
can't be understood from a long history.

He is a huge ball of feelings, that everyone tries to deal with.
It's easy to push but hard to stop.

A Cloudy Sky

I woke up like any other morning,
waiting for the sunlight to come out through my window and
touch my face with its smooth lovely sense of hope…
but there was a different sense today.

The moment I opened my eyes,
I felt something entering my body.
The whole world was cloudy and dark clouds were filling the
sky,
just like they were on a far journey and suddenly came back
to fight the clear sky and take the throne,
as if it heard my prayers for feeling again that day.

There was a gust of wind that was so refreshing, and
romantic in a way it makes your body tremble,
as if it was created for being the most seducing sense for
lovers…
Something words can never express…
What such clouds and wind have on lovers…

I took my morning free-of-sugar coffee, sat along with
Fairuz,

staring at the sky,

feeling something inside my body, something deep but hopeful and lovely

just as a cure for many unknown diseases attacking my body.

I stayed a long time sitting on my window just staring without a single word,

and being far…

so far to even forget my body.

Oh God, what kind of life we are living?

I always ask this question and spend hours wondering. Why are we lost in the crowd of everything?

Why do we think that cloudy weather is sad when it is the opposite?

Cloudy skies are the best and the clearest ever.

They are the transparent image of the true color of the sky.

They are the means to see clearer and deeper.

They have an incredible and confusing way of changing personalities and controlling hearts.

Cloudy skies make my day every time and give a push of hope and happiness.

They are the ones who control colors…

as grey is the one and only fruit of black and white, of pure sadness and pure happiness.

It's what we need to ask for every day.

Colors

Love, blood, and chocolate.

To choose words about love is something hopeless… can't ever find the suitable words that explain it right.

My imagination always goes hunting out for some answers holding my mind in one hand and my heart in another… reaching that place like a white paper full of nothing but waiting to be filled up.

Just like magic is its whiteness, a color that seduces any thought, sentence, word, or idea.
They all sit together on the ground, for the first time ever sticking together like one… waiting.

Behind that white attractive paper, there's a combination of different colors, different levels, bright and dark.

Some killing each other to take place, some hugging like lovers; green and pink.
Some walking as friends; green and brown.

Some standing on the opposite edges; black and white, liking each other, looking at the same place, same end, but never getting close.

Written for them to stay at the end of everything, and once in life, they broke the rules and mingled, had an affair which ended up in a newborn color…a new thought.

A little weird and different one that shines in between, symbolizing power, attractiveness, simplicity, and above all, majesty.

God how much does that innocent whiteness hide different colors.

Different thoughts and ways in mind that express ways in life.

Colors reflect our ways… in a way, they are our thoughts.

Sometimes fighting and sometimes mingling, Sometimes refusing them and always are refusing us. We always wish for and seek what we can't reach.

This is a fact in human beings.

Why can't we just stick to what we can aim for and live in?

We raise a fight in us.

Where black and white stay still, watching and waiting who will take the prize,

and win.

Although, it's the same…

either black or white, both are never clear.

I always paint my thoughts with different colors just to maintain their existence.

And always try hard to find a different color for love, a different thought, a different taste but never found better than the fruit of black and white!

Death

It's exactly the true meaning of life... death and how misunderstood it is.

It's the true image of life.

We live life just to die in the end,
and the sooner we understand, the happier we are in our life.

I may look pessimistic if I think this way, but the fact is that when we see the true image of death, we will appreciate the broken image of the life.

Have you asked yourself what death looks like?
I did, and I saw it scary for the people around me but never for me.

The faster we accept the reality that death lives inside us, the calmer we live our days.

Faces

In this life, it is different to identify faces as they are not the door to the inner soul anymore.

People changed and so did life.

How we see life now depends a lot on appearances, very solid and materialistic views.

We neglect the inner and focus on the outside.

We would love to befriend a girl who follows fashion in all ways.
We would love to befriend a man who spits sugar words all the time.
We would love to befriend a person who keeps on icing us with compliments and telling us what we really aim to be but not always being.

It's the time for faces to glow and show. It's the time for bodies to rule.

It's the time where souls are concealed and hidden sometimes from the person himself to be unconcealed.

It was a long time ago when they said the soul lies in the eyes of a person and you can tell everything about him from a look into his eyes.

Now life has changed and to be close to a person you have to be either like him or a copy of something like him.

And to cope and feel fit, you need to fake and let the wind of change move you.

In the end, don't be sad if people don't recognize you or know the real you but be happy because you never revealed your true self.

Forgiveness

Forgive the perfect look I dress in every day.

Forgive the time I spend every time in wearing makeup, in dressing my body, in decorating my face with different smiles.

Forgive me for being a giving mother all the time.

Forgive me for proving the world that women are tough just as men.

Forgive me for proving you wrong and proving myself right.

Forgive me for all the times I thought I can make it; I can do it and I can feel it…
Forgive me for not knowing how to taste it!

Forgive me for forgetting myself on the path toward being a good woman.

Forgive me for building the outside and ruining the inside.Or maybe the opposite…

Forgetting that the journey starts from down our feet and goes up to our soul.

Forgive me for living on ice knowing that I am made of fire!

Forgive me for letting myself go when all I had to do was to clasp harder and harder.

Forgive me for forgetting my soul behind…
Forgive me for letting the woman inside fade on my way to the female you see every day.

Do you think I deserve your forgiveness? And if I earn it, what difference would it make?

Forgive me… me!

Friendship

It is as what the words consists of… a ship It is meant for you and only you, my friend.
For years, I thought friends can stay in our lives but in fact, friendship stays and friends go…

New friends come in and put a stone in that friendship and leave again.

Friends are memories of times that won't come back.Friends aren't bodies but souls.
Friends are not what we need every day, but it is friendship that we need.

Hanami

A word that takes me years back…

A word that transports me to a fantasy world, to a world that doesn't exist anymore.

A world when I was a princess dressed in white, standing under a cherry blossom tree.

A place when I felt like a hanami, dancing with the wind and letting it touch my silky skin.

A world where my eyes were always looking up and my hands wide open.

Where my body was lighter than a wing.

Where my body was deeply connected with my soul, moving together and understanding each other.

Where I was my own queen and everything in me as unbroken, all new and virgin.

Happiness

What is happiness and how to define happiness?Sometimes, we sit silent for hours,
and squeeze our soul and mind in search for the definition of happiness because recently we are lacking happiness or what they mean by happiness.
People wear happiness all the time for the sake of being happy.

I don't know if they really understand what happiness is and how to be happy.

Life seems to be fake and so materialistic that it blinds us to luxury products and total physical needs.

I look around to find myself among these people,in the same crowd standing there,
lost and cold,
unable to move on…
Stuck maybe in what happiness used to be and waiting with them to understand what has changed and where is that true and innocent and real happiness.

I started to watch their faces, so pale and so fake, laughing all the time.

Very nicely dressed in fancy clothes on and fancy approaches toward life.

Some are very simple and very normal.
I didn't know where to stand and closer to whom, so, I stood alone just in the middle…
In the middle of the crowd and in the middle of all those bodies and under all those souls.

People are so into bodies and don't know how to combine their souls and bodies together.

I asked myself a lot what I am doing here. I know what happiness is and I am happy. So why am I lost here?
Happiness is love even if it's a memory… Happiness is being simple and emotional…
Happiness for me is a couple of hours with the ones I love…
It's in the pleasure of kissing my man and loving him…
It's in the hugs my children give me…
Happiness is in a fancy dinner cooked and served on my table and sometimes.
Happiness is being alone for a few stolen hours of time.
Happiness is when everything seems fine around me, but in the end, am I really happy?

Hidden Figures

Sometimes, we think what we really see is true and what our eyes let us see.

But the fact is that we see what we want to see and not what our eyes let us see.

We decorate what we want to see and give it the touch we need and
ignore what we don't want,
to see even if it is the clearest to our eyes.

We think by this we can protect ourselves and make us happy most of the time,
but we are living in denial most of the time.

We either are not accepting reality or not accepting living the reality.

And in both ways, we are trying our best to adorn all the shabby and weary days we live.

The bodies we react to every day,
the smiles we see no matter if fake or real,the words we hear
every day…
are all the hidden figures.

Jacob

Life is too short…
And who in God's name knows what do these four words mean?

Why is it that a word can't be heard anymore? Why is it that we can't even scream again?
Why is it that our words are turning to be very heavy on our ears and everybody else's?

Why is it that we can't think like before, act like before, smile and laugh like before, or even dream like before?

Why is it that no human can hear that sound but me? That secret deep sound of truth calling every night, that sound coming from deep behind the seven skies,
screaming every night and maybe every hour and every second, calling from between the dark gray clouds as if imprisoned for a long time and now it's free and coming on the back of a huge storm.
Why can't you hear it, human?

Why is it chasing me every night?

Is it fate or a truth or is it reality itself?

I used to talk to myself as if it was always my only friend and
mate.
It was the only true and honest sound that came directly to my
soul.
Myself that never left me, though it was hard on me most of
the times but at the end of the day, it smiled at my
face and whispered some hopeful and good words in my ears.

Now I turn to God.my God…
to ask questions I know I will never have the answers for but
still I'm one of those humans!

God, should I talk about life,pain,
love, sadness,
or even about humansor just about me?

If I talk about love,
I won't ever be clear enough to understand, as the words
needed aren't born yet…
As love is the highest feeling ever that was created since the
first day on this land,
and I can't say that I'm allowed to talk about it,

though it's controlling every single part of me and maybe
ruling me and the ruins inside my soul that were kept for a
long time.

The sound of life calls from every land, it comes on a huge
strong wave,

on the back of a fast black horse racing with the wind.
It comes from the screams of a hungry boy, from the tears of
a lonely old man, from the pain of a tired mother,
from the view of death in a sick man's eyes, from every corner
on this land.

It comes from the smile of a lover who heard his beloved's
voice,
it comes from death and war in this world, it comes from the
highest sky, with every single drop of rain reaching the
ground,
from every laughter of a child.

It comes with the morning breeze that touches the beautiful
shy flowers,
it comes from the screams of a dead man under the ground,
in a sad melody playing all the pains and suffering ever found.
It comes with the sound of crying of a newborn baby, with a
song or a grief, with pain or joy, with sadness or happiness,
with love or hate,
with good and bad,
with the desert and the sea,
it comes from all around you, humans.

Life is a journey and sometimes, it's a mystery unable to be
solved or understood since a very long time.
Since the days of ancient kings and their wars, since the death
of many innocent people because of unacceptable reasons
written and told by ignorant leaders.
Life was a mystery to all of us and to that normal human
named Jacob, who was seeking the true meaning of life and

because of this and to reach his only aim, he travelled all over the land, crossed many seas, and met many other humans on his journey.

Jacob was sitting one day in his small room that was next to his mother's, hearing her breaths and heartbeats, fearing the day she would leave her room and close that only door that was opened for him.

He used to wake up in the early morning, like every day, holding a glass of some fresh milk and a small piece of bread that was baked with some green thyme and enter his mother'sroom with very slow steps.

He used to watch her hands holding the bread, her lips touching the glass, and her half-open tired eyes that were waiting for the eternal rest.
He used to believe that the true meaning of life lay in the soul, body, and eyes of his mother.
Every corner of these two rooms was painted in his mind, every hole in the ceiling, where drops of water fell quickly to join her friends in an old metal pot, every sad and old memory he passed through, every little detail was a picture with a breath in his soul.

Jacob was the only one left for his mother and she was the only light he saw with every second passing in his lonely life. He was far away from reality, in a way he was imprisoned in a world of walls, maybe different colors of walls but still walls where no mouth can speak and no eyes can see and no hand to touch anything, just no senses found, like a dead body found after a long time on a corner of a road.

Though he was far away from reality but, in fact, he was at the middle of the true reality, where he saw everything naked…
naked feelings, hearts, aims, and sometimes naked people with fancy clothes covering their cold fat bodies.

Who can see this reality but him?
Was Jacob imprisoned in his house or was he imprisoned in this life because he saw the ultimate truth, the true colors of skies, the real meaning of a house, the shadows of people walking as fresh.

Was Jacob a real person or just a picture of a human who doesn't exist anymore?
Was Jacob a memory of a true human who passed away with ancient kings?

One day, while Jacob was sitting in his only room, a shadow passed by his window carrying with it the coldest wind ever. Seconds passed and the door was knocked maybe gently or quickly.
Jacob was still staring at the window when he heard the door and walked his few slow steps to open…

There was a man with cold, sharp features standing quietly at the door.
No voice was heard but two big fully opened black eyes were staring.

He entered the house, but his feet weren't touching the floor
as if he was walking in the air.
He came close to Jacob and whispered three words in his ears
that took the light from Jacob's face, gave him the coldest
feeling ever, and left him shocked…

"I am Death," were the words that entered Jacob's ears, body,
and soul…

Jacob couldn't move for a minute or maybe hours.
For some time, he can't count or remember…
"I am Death" were never words but a slap that hit his face and
made him move while standing still in his place.

He realized at the moment that he was there for a reason and
suddenly he knew that the reason of his life was going to leave
him…
the core of his life was going to break,and fade away.

And in a blink of an eye, the body that lived with him in that
small house vanished…
took the soul with him and left nothing but a great emptiness,
and then left.
Jacob was still standing still,eyes wide open,
body cold.

His soul was lost and going in circles above his head…
He couldn't understand what happened and how in a blink of
an eye and as fast as that, a whole human left!
A whole life had just ended.

Journey of Love

A lot of descriptions and symbols are given to love but never to be as fire is to love…

Once a man told me that there are seven stages of love.

To reach the top, you need to burn completely and then, come back in a different shape and color.
He compared it to the journey of fire turning to ash.

The bottom is the moment you light the fire and
with every color it passes through, love goes up a level.

Seven colors and seven levels…
The last level of burning is the highest level of love.

When the fire starts to die, it starts another journey with a different shape and core.

And that is when you reach that sacred level of love.

You feel like a ghost or a shadow flying everywhere that spirit goes.

A Piece of Joy

Sometimes, we don't understand how days are passing without us feeling or counting or even realizing how fast they could be…

Once here or there, we don't know we were wondering about this life, about people and how they changed from the moment they are born.

I keep asking myself how we reached here and how we became this cold.
I look around and all I see is either a lot of colors, or just black.
Sometimes, we feel lost,
we don't know and can't even see the way.

And sometimes, we feel right, and we are the only ones who can lead ourselves on the right track.

Sometimes, we feel like we are sure of nothing in this life.

For me, a woman, and a mother, most of the times I feel secure and safe.

And all this is when I look at my son's face…such an angelic face,
a soft figure,
a perfect creature created by God just for me.
Sent from the highest heavens and highest skies to me…the greatest gift in this mortal life…
How beautiful his eyes are,
a door to an amazing level of joy.

His smile has a magical way of lighting up my days,carrying me up from all this corruption around me. My shore he is and the everlasting hope.
I always wonder how my life would be without him.

The most amazing feeling I felt other than the first love that is still burning in my heart is the moment I felt his heart beating inside my body,
and then I realized that I was looking for that kind of love in my life.

Looking around us, there is nothing worth living,
even that love that we thought we were going to have, that will come to us as an ocean, turned to be a lie.

Just a dream we try to hold on always to pass our days with asmile.

So, keep looking around and we will find the smallest things are the greatest.

Lost

Sometimes, we can't understand ourselves.

We see us floating with wide open arms and eyes staring at something up above.

Sometimes, I die to reach and you're so far away, hiding behind a star maybe.

I know you are staring at me every day with your wide dark brown loving eyes, and your deep manly face…
a face I will never forget.

A face I loved and will always do,
a face that takes my breath away every time I look at or dream of,
a face of a man.
a true and real man.

To be in love is something nice but so painful.

The longing for a touch or a kiss hurts and drags the soul so down;

the missing,the absence,the pain,
all takes out the breath left in the heart.

How can I express how I feel now and that I'm not free
anymore?

A lot is holding me back…
Whenever I try to set my soul free for a moment, I find it
coming back to me crying and asking for peace.

As your place is so far and all I can do is see it from afar but
never to visit again.

My love,
my deep and hidden love…

What can I do to reach to the deep you…?
What can I do to see you again the way I used to…? What
can I do to touch your face,
or to touch mine?

What can I do to know love again and meet love and hold
love?

Just what can I do? I am so helpless now…So weak…

Love

What a shame in life to wake up after a long, long time and find everything's changed.
Look at what has remained inside you, how would that be a moment?

Why is it that everything in life is related to love, which is nicknamed as feelings…?
Always feelings… How mysterious is that! How painful!
And what drives us to madness is that sometimes you hate because you love…

When you find yourself on the top of a mountain and about to fall deep,
you feel like you hate everything, no… everyone!
And reach for a hand to pull you up. That's hate in love,
the pain to reach,
the hate to fall in love.

Love is selfish!
It always keeps asking for more and more,
till you reach a time that you can't handle love inside you. It always has a way in driving you crazy,

like being very happy, just as drunk, and very depressed, sad, and confused.
You won't ever be normal again.It's just like a curse…
A different curse, created by God, and comes to you from the most beloved people.

And when your tears die to fall,
you search for the pain inside you and can't even know where!
Really deep…
through your blood, bones, organs…squeezing your heart…
torturing you, even in the way you breathe…choking you,
putting over your breath a heavy pain and then you feel like you hate your body.
It becomes your prison.

If I knew that love is the shortest way to sadness and the longest way to happiness,
I would have announced it as a forbidden way.

What a way!
You walk and walk looking at the happiness in the end as a shining light for your life…
and still you walk and with every step there's a fall,

just like the sparkling of that light strengthens you and pulls you up again to walk.
But the real question is, will you reach it?
Still, I've thought that I'd be the first one to leave.Never felt this before,
lonely and tortured, lost and deeply sad. But still, that light is always pulling me up.

For all my life I cherished the butterfly…

beginning from the word as it sounds when I say BUTTERFLY.

It makes me alive.

I always wished to be a butterfly,

so colorful, filled with life and love given for all and a reason for creating a smile on others' faces.

Moments

To be in this world is something tough.
You keep running by the act of breathing to reach,
But in reality, you are still in your place, feeling you've crossed shores,
roads, ways, seas, and skies,
but if you look down at your feet, you'll find yourself never moved.

Guess that's the meaning of life.
What a shame…
full of ups and downs.

To know what you want is something hard and hopeless.
It takes you forever to know and decide… an extremely hopeless situation.

And when it comes to love…
You'll find yourself living in two worlds.
One of them that keeps on dragging you inside, asking always for more and more till you become a slave…

To think about life is a very hard thing…
full of many things.

I can't think about anything but sadness, hurt, tears, secret
love,
dying hearts, lost eyes, flying souls,
the world of bodies, and the ending of life.

You run and run and run and, in the end, either you reach, or
you lose after reaching.
People are bad!
Their real souls are just living outside their bodies, watching
them sadly and waiting a moment to feel strong. To feel sad
is something not nice and painful,
but still naturaland without it,
I think people won't even know what feelings are.

Moments always die the second they are born, and once the
breath of life screams, it dies!
Everything becomes memories of moments… What to feel!
Every time I feel like a stranger in a strange world and when
I open my eyes on beautiful coming things, a little painful
thing comes my way and throws me in the middle of
memories.
Questions with no answers, words and words.

It's just that I'm losing myself in the crowd of words and
memories…

Looking around, I find many people in this huge crowd but
none to talk to!

Wings…
I always wished to have wings,to fly over the world,
look into eyes…
wonder where the meaning of life lies.

In the blink of an eye
lies the secret of the world,
where the world ends and begins in a moment! The secret of
dying and living at the same time.Look at people,
at their lives,
at the blink of their eyes, wonder where the hell am I!

To live and die at the same time,to love and hate,
to hope and lose, all at the same time.

To be yourself and feel another one just living inside your
body,
acting instead of you.

Well, life is a mystery moved by human beings.
Sometimes, I feel so much like talking but unable to move my
tongue.

My Heaven

To define heaven is like sitting in a room with extremely white walls and no color interferes with white.

A room with no noise and no people and no hands.

A room in which you feel you own every minute that passes in, and every space lived and every breath taken.

This is what comes to mind when you think of peace in heaven,
but that's not my heaven.

My heaven exists when I lay my eyes on yours,that face…
and that beard…
feels at that time how blessed I am with such a man I don't get to know enough.
A man I struggle to know what exactly he loves to give…
what exactly he thinks of, to share, and what exactly he imagines living…
with him and to him…

Not just like any other woman, I try to keep my man for
having a man in my life… the fact is, I love having you as my
man…
the man…
in my life is something great for me sometimes to digest.
You made me feel incomplete most of the time,
so short to reach that wall of yours.

You gave me broken wings that take me nowhere, but far from
you…
You scattered my soul and lost it in the crowd of your
masculine appearance.

You painted me in your own colors and left me alone on a
river.

You took my soul, raised it up and left it there… wiped it
clean and clear…
and kept above your head.

You put transparent chains around me to keep me locked
andcontained into you.

You wrote my life and still do, and I know can't be without
you,
played it smart so I'll be yours and took all my strength and
replaced it with pure love and need—
a need for you, my man.
You framed me your woman and that's how it will always be.
Just the other hidden side of my heaven on earth.

Nature

When dreams hunt your world, rule your mind, and control your heart and soul…

When they come to you whenever the night falls and put on the whole world a beautiful dark dress, adorned with shinning little sparkles that look so attractive in anyone's eyes…

When dreams just stand in front of your eyes trying to move you, make you talk, and breathe life inside you,
fill your eyes with hope,
and you just act as a person with a dead body breathing something in this weird life you don't even know.

Then you put dreams in a mail envelope and send them back to the skies, give it a chance to fly and float along with stars, to shine like them.
And there you are…
staring at them far from you, like a treasure and you tell yourself,
there they will be safe, better than carrying them with your soul and body in this sick world with its sick people.

Our world is going down to somewhere we don't wish to know, live, or even see.

Trees are growing everyday with their deep green colors, sometimes naked, just preparing themselves for a nicer dress, full of colors, and decorated by those Japanese cherry blossoms that still fill the sky with a sacred touch of magic that goes deeply inside each loving soul and gives it a touch of simple and real life.

The sea is still as high and deep as it was always... sometimes calm when listening to people's complains and pains with no blame...
always big and ready to hear more.
His chest is open for any injured, friendless person or just one like me, lonely but not alone,
with many people around.

Maybe it's better to be alone than lonely and having many around,
where time is your killer holding a sharp knife ready to kill anything that goes in your way.

How powerful time is!
Sea is God's gift to us...
the place where we can throw everything no matter how big, shameful, or simple...
if it has affected deeply our soul.
The place where everything in us is set free!

Sea is our imagination, the only place in us that no one ever touched…

It's where we can spread our wings and fly…and really fly.
Choose our mate, draw him as we've ever dreamt of, pick up our favorite colors, decorate our ways with weird simple attractive flowers.

Give him a touch of life that mingles with the deepest place inside his soul,
breathe him, simply give him life, and where he can give us a simple touch.

A touch… that erases all pains and signs of traveling between worlds.
A touch that can mingle inside with our veins, visit the heart, throw some flowers on its door and unlock it behind.
A touch that carries our deep breath outside our body with every single pain…
Just releasing everything.

How powerful these things are…?

Just like a kings' highness and majesty who gives orders and commands,
and everyone is on their knees with a smile… Every natural thing is still the same.

Sand and water, the beauty of sunset, the colors of trees and flowers.

Everything that makes the world beautiful.

BUT only what makes it sick and disgusting sometimes is people themselves.
They changed everything from the moment they touched the ground.

If you be yourself everywhere and with everyone, you'll be weird and an alien.

There's a scene in a film called "Angle Eyes".
 I would never forget how much romantic and deep it was…
Where the lovers were bathing in a river,
and water,
the purest gift ever created, was falling on them, touching their bodies,
erasing every single unclear and true thing in their souls…
giving a chance for their feelings to be naked in front of each other…
Nothing inside is hidden…Just naked feelings.

They were just laughing like innocent babies. It's a high sense of love not found anymore, just him living in her eyes,

made her hold the sadness and loneliness in his eyes close to her and with a simple kiss that pulled all his pain out of his body…
and he goes down kissing her feet!
A place that has never been touched by anybody's lips…

That was a scene symbolizing naked deep love.

Jibran Khalil, the famous writer, once said, "I'd like to be always a bee that licks the honey from your feet."

Would that be exaggeration or is it a different kind of love?

How can a woman be in that highness for a man nowadays?

How can he be her own only special life that she breathes for him and breathes him to understand all his pains and takes them out?

I always ask myself why do I go deep in such romantic deep movies?

They have magic on me, just controlling me,

Those have a different story and symbols that control my imagination,

and make me ask a question when will I ever go down to earth and live my real life?

Or is it we women ask for a lot or ask for a fantasy life?

Can't it be both?

Why when we talk or think about these stories, they slap us in our face with some harsh words as "be real… these are only movies."

Just why can't it be both?

Why is it hard for a man to try to give some touch of fantasy to their relationships and enjoy the sweetness of life that would bring to their own!

If they would only know the magic of it and the power…

The fact that it's their game and it is the only way for them to rule and be their majesty.

But I've heard of few,
very few who understood that…
and I guess it takes us back to the top.
It's men's nature and hard to break the rules.

Sunlight

What a wonderful moment to feel the sun touching your skin
and even burning you… making you feel alive,
reminding you of one of the sources of life although inside
you, life is on the edge just waiting for a blow to fall.
What a silly feeling!

But what can you do if you always try hard to escape it but
still it's inside living on your organs like a bacterium?

I had been looking at the sunlight hard till I could not see
anything more…
and the scene of a memory came to my mind.

I felt it with open eyes, and I even saw you sitting next to me,
really as if you weren't far and between us were seas and lands
and countries and people and faces and eyes…
I was trying hard to breathe but something was just in my
throat, blocking the air…

So much love lives inside us really and the lovers are such
poor people…
we see some blaming themselves,

some crying with a knife in their hearts squeezing and enjoying the scene of blood everywhere with a loud smile.

Some are laughing at pain, running away, they look like those who face the monster with a loud laugh as if they know they're about to die and want to die with a laughter that kills.

Some sitting and eating,drinking,
living,
and breathing even from their memories.

They are living and taking strength from memories with hope as their partner in everything.

Why do we always run for something we don't fully know or understand?
We all know we belong to some place, but the question is, to where and to what?

We keep searching inside us for an answer.Can that place be a human being?
For me, I think every creature aims for the place he belongs to, and this place is a person who's nearer to the heart than the veins themselves…
a person that eats with you without even inviting, a person who drinks with you without asking…
a person who lives in the cells of your blood with your deep love feeding him and making him bigger and older,
a person you can name a soul partner sharing everything,

entering any place inside you and walk between your heart, brain, mind,

kidneys, stomach, hands, eyes, neck, liver, the veins in your legs and hands…
all your organs…
and you stand watching and feeling him more and more and more…
and even giving him way to pass and play wherever he wants. Isn't it strange!

He can control everything in you… make you feel warm in cold,
and cool in hot
and secure in the time you are afraid, and fulfill your thirst and hunger.

You feel like there's a workshop for building inside you…
Dreams are built with lovely colors and butterflies all around.

On This Day

On this day, I do remember you…

On this day from years ago, I celebrated you.

On this day years ago, the precious gift you would have liked from me was just a close smile I wear.

To look at how years can pass so fast is so scary and weird… days are passing by us without us feeling alive.
We eat and drink, work and run all day, have sex occasionally and ask ourselves every night before closing the dreaming eyes what was the happy moment we had today?

The fact that we pretend happiness is so scary and pathetic, while we say to others and ourselves that this is what life is meant to be…

As a woman of these days…
and I would stop at the word woman for a while. I'm a working mother till afternoon who has the most sacred and transparent job ever… yet the hardest job.

I'm a mother…

a very loving wife who sees her man… a man, regardless of the differences and the ongoing and endless conversations about him changing to what I need or the missing things in him or me…

He is my man.

I do lose hope sometimes and search for a meaning in my day other than living for my kids and supporting my husband.

What do I need? What makes me happy? Did I get what I dreamt of?

I learned it the hard way…

that no one can ever make you or give you happiness and happiness is something you should earn and give to yourself.

Sometimes, being alone with my coffee, and a good book to read is what makes me happy,

but even this only lasts for hours, and I go back wondering again about happiness.

And here comes today, a day like any day that holds a day with him and so on…

a day that you can imagine and expect all night and wake up hoping for…

a day in which you will fulfill what you want or a day that can take you down so much that you can't even breathe.

And this is life…

no matter how you want to imagine it or believe it is, it will never change,

as it will always be full of surprises.

It never defines you or has any relation with your fate or luck.
Life has its own ups and downs…
in which it will take you according to the wave.

I stand there sometimes wondering about my life later and how will it be, and I feel so afraid of the coming…
I am afraid of losing on all sides,
I am afraid of sadness as I can't face it and I will not know how to face it.

Sometimes, I feel I want to…
Simply I search in my day for a hope to make me smile for tomorrow…
A smile from my kids or a time to spend alone with my coffee or a gathering in my house and I cook…
and sometimes a breakfast I spend with my small family, a breakfast that my kids call family time.

And yes, whatever happens today, we still have tomorrow…
I totally believe in this, and I try hard to believe and live by this.

Sometimes, it's what your eyes can tell you…
as sometimes, you see life as simple and nice as a passing day and sometimes, you look around and all you can see is sadness, very dull faces and people running and running to an end they can't see or find…
and when the sound of life calls and shouts, you stop and look at yourself.
You'll be shocked at the heavy load you are carrying on your shoulders.

I absolutely have no answers for anything I ask myself, but I try hard to give myself answers that give me peace and a way to move on.

I used to fight for what I wanted and now I believe that everything is meant to be and there is no use of running toward the unknown,

or fighting to gain or change.

Marriage is a very complicated relation and yet so beautiful and deep.

But you still feel there's always something missing, that flame, that fire…

but it seems that when we own something we wanted for a long time, the flame dies once you have it,

and then the dilemma of lighting it again is so hard.

Love is there and the need is there, but that fantasy kind of love is pushed hard to the reality of marriage.

But this is how men are.

They don't know how to act in such situations, and they never think of being warm.

And here comes the importance of leaving your man for a couple of days.

Men can get lost without their women and the fact is that they don't admit or realize it until it's real.

If you hear stories from different women about different situations,

you'll understand by comparing it to your story that all men
are the same…

I won't say same mentality but same structure,
and you find yourself in the end surrendering to the fact that
it's them and nothing you can do that would change that.

Options

What we choose is not always what we mean to have or to live.

What we have is not always what we need or want.

What we live is not always what we wished for or what we dreamed of.

Where we are now is not always where we want to be.

What we feel now is not what we really want to show to the world.

What I want to do now is far from what you see me doing.

The way I want to move, and dance is never even close to the way I walk and talk.

We are all in masks all the time…by choice or by force, in the end it's the same.

We are trapped somewhere that doesn't define us.

It's either one of two…
our soul dragging our body or our body dragging our soul.
It's never the two of them in one place… they are suffering, each one alone… and we are suffering with them.
They are never to meet,never meant to mingle.

Pain

Pain…
what a very short word that carries huge and heavy meanings.
Pain…
isn't just a feeling or a word to describe yourself or to even use it when you want to.
It's larger and heavier than it sounds.
Pain…
is sometimes love and sometimes hate.
Pain…
is prison and freedom at the same time. It's the road and the end.
It's the land and the gate.
Pain…
is happiness and sorrow. Is the heart and the mind.
Is the body and soul… is you and me… only you and me.
Pain is everywhere and in all,
it's born the moment we come to this life,born with us,
born with the first tremble and the very first sound of us as humans.
Pain escorts us and guides us in every stage of our lives.

Pain was and is always with us,we can even see it and feel it.

It was in the first laughter you saw on your mother's face, in your father's voice,
in your walking for the first time or crying or playing. It was there the first time you loved or felt growing.
It was there the first time you looked at yourself in the mirror and knew you are changing.

Pain was there when you left school and your parents and your whole life and stepped into a new one.
Pain was there when you hugged your mother or kissed your father,
when you sat in your grandma's lap or next to your grandpa's legs,
pretending to be happy without you knowing that it may be the last time you will see them.
Pain was there, hiding…It was there all the time.
And the day you left your parents' house, how happy it was to start a new life.
Pain was guiding you and you were blind to see and feel, there's nothing called going on…
It's only leaving something completely and stepping into a new thing.
A new unknown thing.
And there was pain filling every part of you.
Pain is the point…
the string that connects all to all… heart to mind, body to soul,
happiness to sadness,

black to white, water to soil.
Pain was there in the first kiss, just the first time…

It's there in the warmness of the kiss and in the highness of a kiss.

Pain was there in the first time you sat next to your love, embraced and hugged and loved.

Pain was there when you knew that was your limit and you can't go further,

you can't move from there.

You want him badly and want to enter that fantasy world with him, but your legs and your body won't allow you.

You have boundaries and limits and there comes pain…with all its glory and its majesty,

come to live inside you and torture you every day,

comes to invade your soul and close every door and build a huge gate that you won't be able to open again.

Pain was there in all your moments,

even when you smiled at the memory of your love… it's there.

Pain is what was feeding your soul for many years, and you thought it was bad days that you will move on later…

Pain was there.

I saw it.

I talked to it.

I met it and I felt it so deep,dressing the best,

showing its best, and talking its best.

Pain can control your feelings and leave you in a trance even in your hardest times,

pain can squeeze your heart.

I was there standing still unable to move or look around. I was frightened, cold, and alone,
wanted to shout but couldn't raise my voice and speak a word,
wanted to turn around but nothing was there except shades of white and grey,
wanted to walk but was heavy.
I stayed in my place and felt like it's the end…but the end of what?
The end of being alone or the end of being in love or the end of being alive?
I couldn't answer myself,couldn't do anything.
All I know,
is that pain is killing me inside.

It's harder and heavier than I can carry inside me all the time.
I try to take some shots of happiness and hopes but still they are weak in front of it.
I'm lost and feeling so fatigued.
Once I dreamt and imagined myself sitting on a cloud. Up there a cloud,
so white and so high and light.
Me sitting there was a dream that hunted me every day and I imagined myself looking down at me and my life… what would I change and what would I do,
where would I go and what could I replace. How I can reach that feeling and escape pain!

It's my,your,
and everyone's destiny to be tortured by pain and many faces of pain.

Pain is there when you choose a dress that suits your body.
It's there in the question you raise about the beauty of your body or your face or your smile or your soul.
It's there in every smile and every laughter,
but our eyes and mind deny the truth that it exists, and we tryhard to feel and live the opposite.
Pain is there when a miserable woman fakes her life to show others and herself the best image of life lived.
Pain is there always and even when it's not there,it's there.
Pain is higher than we think and powerful than we can defeat.
It conquers every minute of our lives and controls us,
wears a hidden mask and strolls around us.

Shapes of Love

I never knew that love can be defined in many forms and many shapes.
It came to me with different abstract colors.

I never knew that I would experience love in its many forms until,
I was brought down to the bottom surface of feelings and that was the highest I reached in all my life.

Once I believed that love can be so emotional,
a feeling that takes you higher than higher and I used to see love as a deeper connection between a soul and a body.

It used to be a dream and I had a lot of hopes hanging there, but the fact that love can change and dress in colors shocked me to the bottom.
Love used to exist in the core of our bodies.
It is a message felt and seen in the very first moment.
Something unexplainable happens at that moment.
When it attacks, it hits the body first with that tremble that flips your heart from its place,

and suddenly, your vision becomes clear, the sky becomes gray, and your senses sharpen.

It is a moment when time stops, and you feel reborn again at the spot.

When you realize, for the first time, the reason for your existence on this earth.

Love comes as a package.

Like Santa who keeps showering you with gifts that can lift your spirit high every time.

At that very moment, every word will carry a meaning starting from the world.

The feeling of belonging to something or someone is what every human starves for.

Being in this life for some time I learned that there's a thin line between love and attraction.

You mistake attraction whether physical or emotional with love.

Attraction comes in the same way as love, but it lasts for a definite time.

It comes with numbered days and hours, with one color, with few words only, and with only one shape.

It has no power neither on the body nor on the soul.It attacks fast and sneaky.

Sometimes, attraction is unexplainable also.

The way it attacks and the person it comes with is vague.

Sometimes, when you feel attracted to someone who is not your type,

in any time, is mysterious.

The funny fact about it is that you are fully and continuously aware of
its mortal state,
but for some reason, it gives you a push for every day, a glow that you missed on the way,
and a smile you need in your day.
That attraction fills some empty blanks and gives a temporary hope for tomorrow.
Sometimes, we need a push, a feeling even if it's a fake one but we still aim and chase it.
That attraction comes in a shape of something missing in our life,
and if we are smart enough, we will be able to identify the blank and try to fill it…
and if we aren't that lucky, we chase that attraction thinking about it every moment, asking ourselves about reasons, knowing that sooner it will be gone.
By that time, it won't even leave a scar as it hasn't even touched the core.
The core that can categorize all feelings and put them in the right order.
The core that every human is afraid of facing, seeing, and feeling.
That core has the only power that can control us all… body and soul.
I wondered how thin is that line between attraction and love.
Many people fall for it until they find themselves at the top.
So shallow and so quiet.
The funny thing is that they know the time to leave and depart that space and they wait for it.

Love can fool a person and mistake him with many faces and masks and only those who are lucky on this earth can find that sacred love and allow it to conquer every organ from inside to outside.

Love has been the main dilemma in every human being's life. It has been the question people try hard to find answers for but fail.

Men, especially men, keep on ignoring the word love as if they are afraid of it.

The fact that they understand the word and identify their needs scares them to the limit that they deny feeling it or chasing it. The way men need love is more than they understand.

The moment they realize how love can change them, they panic as they won't be able to control their actions or needs or even their bodies.

The Garden of Words

So many words to describe this killing noise. So many words are there to get kicked off.

So many words are there to end the silence or to start it, I'm not sure.

But I'm sure that there are so many words in this silence. In a blink of an eye, words gather inside,

creating a pile.

It was always words and words that control us, whether on the inside or on the outside.

Words and words are all what we need to have and own. As words sometimes are our biggest enemy.

They can fail us, and they can save us.

They say we can control the words that leave us, but sometimes, words control us and shape us.

In a society that depends on images and appearances, words are confused and are unable to leave in peace.

Words can live inside and eat us sometimes if not released to the outside to breathe.

Words can break our heart and the more time they stay in, the angrier they become.

We must acknowledge the fact that words are to be treated nicely.

We must give them some space and show them the life sometimes so they can show us the good and healthy face of life.

Time

This day seems to begin like the others,
but my mind was there beyond Fairuz and her stories. For the first time I was far from her,
I was there all alone.

I met Time,
stared at him for a time!
And then so many questions came to me in front of him, and he was just cold and scary…
a giant to me with weird features and sharp endings.
Just as me entering a weird house asking the gatekeepers where this place is…
Where the hell am I?
How long was the way up to here and how long will it take me to reach back to my place?

And it was amazing to have a little conversation with Time.
I sat there on the ground, staring at Time again with his big open eyes…
just wondering where the way to the shore is,
just being there watching the sun as it dies, touching the sand and water…

the two sources of life,
how matching they both are…both kill and give birth…
like heart and mind…. matching but each by itself.

I looked again at Time,
asked how he can control our lives, our memories, our
feelings,
our bodies…
What kind of power does he have on everything?

And how and why everything is attached to him?
He just looked at me with cold, cold eyes and answered me
by a simple hard sentence,
"Life is a period of time and time is the hand that moves life,"
and turned away from me.

I stood there alone, couldn't speak a word…
and at that moment, I knew I had to go back in life to believe
and see my position in it now,
and to understand the way I am.I went back walking,
and suddenly, found the shore…sand and water
matching insideheart and mind
where the heart is bigger and have some corners and weird
unreachable places
closed doors
but an open gate!

I think it's hope…
to be a complete match.

Now I know everything in life takes time,but Time still takes
time no matter what.
And I have to hold on…
hold on carrying everything with me.
Just a huge world living insideand so much joy is there…
a white different bright
bright light always shines in the end…but still needs Time!

A Woman

To be a woman is hard…
a sentence we have all heard many times and for many reasons
and claims and facts…

But the truth is, being a woman is complicated but not hard,
is simple but not easy,
is clear but not understandable.

We women were raised to praise men, even to draw our lives
in theirs,
don't know if it is in our biological form or we were just
taught to be like this.

We analyze our beauty and sacrifice our days and print our
hours for the sake of attracting them,
for the sake of looking good as they say.

We fear their absence in our lives, and we crave their attention
and love.
We live a day to see that look in their always wide-open
eyes and to hear a sweet word that makes us smile even
though we

know it's sometimes so fake but we make the best of it and turn it into a memory we keep on for some drought days.

Before marriage, you feel the power of you and enjoy that pinky colored life with all its beauty.
You wake up happy and sleep in a dream.
You feel him always around and you'll fall for it every single day,
ready for everything and anytime.

And then you find yourself asking the woman inside you just everyday what changed and who changed?
Is it us or is it life?
Or we just don't understand that life and got lost in our feelings and moved by them!

There were days where we felt like nothing just next to our men.

When we rushed to get the best of all,
turned ourselves into machines to keep on the track and not lose a minute.
A day where we forgot ourselves but took care of ourselves,
forgot that we are body and soul,
and that body and what you put on is but a reflection of your soul.
We dressed differently and acted differently and faked a smile or a life or a character for the sake of fitting in his world!
This is us now! But when will we change?

To You

To open my eyes to you,a thing never did before.

It's weird what it feels now…

as if it's not me and it's hard to fight this feeling, it's controlling me.

I wonder for the first time why do I love you? Why do I deeply love you?

Is it because you are the type of man, I dreamt about for like all my life?

Or is it because deep inside you, I know there's a kind heart and loving soul?

Where do I begin?How do I begin?

Let me start by saying how I love you and I can't imagine anything without you.

At the very beginning, you were a different man,so open to me.

I used to see those naked feelings,

your hands used to hug mine all the time, your lips were always thirsty for my kisses, those kisses which I really miss…

those loving kisses that used to follow my lips all day and at any time.

Oh, where should I begin?

Maybe you didn't know me for real, you didn't see the real me.

Now I wake up to new questions. What did I think you looked like?

Was it always like that and I was blind to see all? And now I'm looking at you,

or should I say staring at every part of you… sitting on that sofa,

just lazy to move your eyes,

drawing a very simple smile on those adorable lips.

I know nobody on earth loved you the way I did and still do and will always do,

but now with you, I'm missing a lot of things… I'm missing me being a woman,

with all these heavy things on my shoulders dragging me down and down just to the deepest,

to wake up unable to move and look at my face.

Sometimes, I wish I can run for just a day, far away from everything and everyone.

Sometimes, I dream of going back to a girl, just a simple girl in her parents' house…
Irresponsible.

Have nothing to think about except what my mom will cook and what time I'll wake up for some chatting,
or maybe shopping…

Oh, so many things which I can't do now.

It may be the end but sometimes, it's just the beginning.I felt like a tree,

a fruitful one.

With all that care I hadfrom the sky,

she betrayed me and went away to a place I couldn't even imagine.

Everything in me died with her. I lost my leaves and my seeds.

With God's care, I still own the roots which were the base she made as strong as my hope was…

and still…

and I know that my tree will blossom one day and when it does, it will be for her, because of her and only her.

It's deep in the soul where our life lies and where secrets live and feed…

though there's a touch of madness in every aspect of our lives.

A touch is the simplest message sent to the heart,

but how hard is it to find the way to the heart, and how simple it is?

You just can't ask… it's a way you walk in and through without your will.

It's a way that drives you to wonder and ask questions you've never thought of,

beginning by finding so many hidden beautiful things that you forgot they existed and lived deep in you.

A weird way that takes you higher with stars and within seconds makes you a slave.

It's always the same path for men and women,

although the view is different, and the main sex is different. A Letter from every woman to her husband…

Tribute to My Grandma

We all spend time searching and aiming for peace of mind and soul.

We can sit for hours thinking deeply about life, going far enough even from ourselves.

Sometimes, running away from days, moments, and people.

We ask ourselves several times in a minute, what is life…?

The most mysterious question ever…

Sometimes, life means a person…

a unique person, a different one, a complete figure, full of colors,

unlimited lines, deep painting… it's a man, a true man ever created,

it seems to be that it lies in the eyes and hands of a man.

It seems like sometimes our lives

pass in front of us without us noticing, or thinking deeply about it.

Many things act seriously in our passing days,

making us ask such weird questions, we're even unable to answer…

and sometimes pushing us away, making us live on that surface, breathing just to keep alive, eating and drinking to be alive,

acting to be alive and not living to be alive.

I always used to say, 'Live for living and not for being alive'.

God!

I lived a very different life,a separated one,

it was hidden deep inside, and a great event brought everything out.

Women

I keep wondering why women want to be equal with men?
Why would they fight to be like them or act like them…?
work like them or sleep or dress or speak like them?

Why would they ask for so little when they already have a lot?

Why would they think that men have something they all desire, need, or want?

While in fact they have nothing women can't and don't do.
Moreover, they have nothing to do that women aren't capable of.

Being a woman is a gift for us, though we totally think the opposite.
I never wished to be a man but almost acted and pretended to be and handled everything like a man.

We were totally wrong to think that men are born to be the strongest creatures,
and can handle the hardest things and face them.

We think that if we try to push ourselves harder and put heavy loads on our shoulders, then that will make us look stronger and maybe secure and safe.

But life corrected our beliefs and showed us a different way and led us to the real world of a woman.

Now I call myself a woman of my time, proudly, I say and happily, I act, silently, I take…
and loudly, I prove it.

A woman that knows what she wants and what she needs to get in time, it's hard to see what is out there for her.

A woman that kept a world in her heart and never showed it to any now feels the wings growing inside and there will be a time when she must fly and set everything free.

A woman whom I call the strongest in time when there is so much to handle.

A woman whom I call the softest, in time she was meant to be the shelter.

A woman whom I call the purest, in time everything around is just a lie and all the people seem to have many faces for one body.

A woman whom I call a wing, a bed, a cover, and a drink,

a bridge and a road,
a fast way and a hidden way,
a huge life and a very small world…
a woman of anytime that can bring you your time at any time.

Today, I know what a woman is and how and why I can call myself a woman of my time.

And now it's time to wake up and see it deeply… We don't need clothes or brands to look pretty.
We don't need a lot of exercise and style and modern ways and clothing to show the beauty inside and focus more on how people will see it.

It's time to take care of our souls as they are the mirrors and the doors for the world.

It's time to realize how a woman should be these days, how she should talk and act and dress smart.
It's time for men to see a different woman now,
to wake up from their dreams about old women who they think are weaker in handling life issues and still throw on their shoulders the heavy,
heavy loads of life.

And in the end, they come around to say she is a woman! She's not meant to be strong.

So how in hell did you give her all those responsibilities and allowed her to manage your house and your body?

It's time for all you women out there to realize the power hidden inside and bring it out.

Don't wait for a man to give wings to fly.

Don't wait for a day that will bring you happiness, go and make it yourself.
Create a moment of joy for yourself.
It's okay to lose control sometimes and to forget some of your responsibilities.
It's okay to act weird or to act as you are supposed to be.

God and all gods out there now and back in time cherished women and saw her as the chest,
as the house and the shelter,
so, act like that… don't be the door and be the house itself.

Don't be the shore where he can lay and be the sea itself, huge and free.

Don't be the image and be the subject,
ignore all the signs and take those who lead you to happiness.

Understand and digest the woman inside you and give her what she deserves.
We need men but not to live for,
we need them to live with… to share and not to give.
We don't need them to complete us, we are perfect as created.

If only we open our eyes wider to see the pure us, the strong us, and the power we have…

We put men as our aim,as our destination,
but, in fact, they are the journey to our destination.

They are the hand that should guide us and protect us but not
who takes us there.

Men should be our help but not our ride.

Show no fear, women, and enjoy being a woman for once.It
was and will always be our game and our rules.

A Dream

Today I saw you and I saw your face just so close to me. I was shivering deep inside and trying to memorize the details of your face. The way you do your hair and your big hazel eyes. You were sitting there but your eyes never met mine. I was screaming on the inside for a look into my eyes so I can tell you how much I miss you and how easily you can rock my world.

You are the only shake that my body needs to bring out the woman inside.

You are the only one that can hurt me and heal me at the same time.

You have the power to pull me back to earth and you are the only one who has the power to give me wings to fly.
You were once the reason I called myself a woman and you are now the reason why I lost that woman inside.

A World of Mine

I am dreaming… and dreaming only these days.

Living in a world of my own… a world that I built or maybe trapped in for so long now.

A world where everything is okay, and I live the way I want. A world where I can be myself without limits and judgments. A world that has only me and myself, but, and yes, there is always a BUT in everything in this life.

My world has me and I have you! You are scattered inside me, and you are there in every breath I take.

Nothing was ever enough to take me out and free me. My soul is still wounded, and nothing healed it.

That wound is still bleeding and that is why I am trapped in that world…

I am dreaming or maybe living… I lost track of time and reality.

I am living in a world and there's another world within my soul!

I hear you calling me every time I am down, but I can't reach for your hand to pull me up. You are there, I can feel you, but I can't see you. You are there, I know it, but life has treated you badly and I wasn't better than life. I can see you standing there wounded too but stuck like me and there's a deep valley in between us. I know you are watching the days pass and you are trapped too.

Dream, my love, dream like me… live with me in that world because we only exist there.

Gravity

I am so lost in my life, and I don't know how to give definition to anything anymore.

I feel like I lost interest in everything and nothing has the power to attract me.

I don't know if I can go back to being the same person.

I look down at my body and it proves to me right most of the time that I did lose myself somewhere out there and it seems impossible to me to find it anywhere no matter how hard I try.

I hate my own skin and I wish most of the time to change but changing is not as easy as it sounds.

I can't push myself to change or do more as I feel I have the world over my shoulders.

Time seems to be so mean to me… it's passing fast and holding my days with it. I do try to chase it but there is no point; it's so strong and controls all around me.

I'm floating most of the time and no matter how hard I try; I can't reach the ground though I try to hold on to anything that makes me feel heavier but there's no definition for gravity in my life now. I am so fragile like a feather carried by any gustof wind.

I ask myself every single day what life is and why do we have to do this and what did I put myself in?

I don't know but can't find meaning for anything now. I know I am just living and working under many titles. I used to know how to define happiness and now I can't even tell if it is a myth!

I know that it has something to do with family or parents, but I can't really define it. I think there's a strong connection between gravity and happiness.

Silence

The world suddenly is so quiet. Silence is filling all the blanks and taking over time.

Silence is all what you hear now and life in a blink turned into hours and minutes and sometimes days.

Grey took control of the sky and hid all colors.
The only thing you can see standing up high is those trees with their blossoms. People are back to earth for the first time in a very long time.
Masks are no longer a mystery and eyes no longer meet eyes.

Bodies are lost and laying so down, so close to earth. For the first time, bodies are mingling with earth and waiting for a drop of water to rise again.

The walls and houses are holding memories of yesterday… memories of a hidden dream or a hope of tomorrow.

For the first time, there is no chaos in the world and no turning points, and I find myself again so calm in this silence.

We've never believed that time can control us and now time has proven to all that it is the master of all.

We need time to heal and time to breathe. Time to rise and time to live.

Time to break the silence and time to give life to all hopes and dreams hidden inside.

Time to raise up the spirit of earth.

Time to fix what is broken and time to dream again.

Time to decide if it is the end or if there's more that life would offer us.

We need time to pass time.

Time to pray and time to be forgiven.

Freedom… to be free is something indescribable. Freedom is not only for bodies but for minds too.

The ability to be free in our thoughts and to be in control of our thoughts and hopes is freedom itself.

Fragile

A leaf, once hanging on a big tree, with a sudden gust of wind falls and joins her friends to be thrown and flown away… eventually disappearing and fading.

That's when death comes in its glory and picks it up to take on an eternal journey, we decide its path when we were at our glory.

Death has no master as is the master of all. Death is a master on its own.
We keep running from him and he laughs in our faces and takes us in a blink.

That's when life seems so short and shocks us with its fragility.

We keep running after life and life was never meant to be lived.
We are prisoners in this world and the world keeps showering us with temptations and fancy and livable days.

Life is about memories… very short memories of moments we lived or live.

Moments of people who touched us deeply and left. Not because they want to but because they are meant to. They are meant to give us that deep feeling of loss so we can rememberand look at death.

Bound

Life is all about choices and we are bound to every choice we make in this life.

Choices we make are tied to us and sometimes define the person we became. We pass through a lot of journeys and experiences that leave us in unwanted places and images of characters that once were far from being us.

We live pretending that this is the new us, but in fact we are running away from the truth that we changed to what life wants us to be or what people we live with want us to be.

The question that we ask ourselves every day is, are we happy with what we became?
Are we happy with the person we are living in?Is it what we want to be?
Does this version of a woman that what we want to show to everyone and to ourselves?
Who are we changing for?
Who are we going to hide our true self from and why?

Many questions we ask every day when we look in the mirror. That mirror that reflects nothing but what it sees. It never lies and never shows us what we want to be but shows us what we became. That mirror is our judge and wakeup call.

We start asking, finding answers to fill in the blanks inside but nothing can be done. We suddenly feel trapped in that mirror that reflects the choices who made us the women we are in our present days.

You start counting the blessings of what this new version of a woman has brought to your life. You start questioning and arguing with yourself, trying to soothe the pain inside and sometimes convincing it that it is the life we want and what we are hiding and missing is way less than what we have.

And here comes the daily struggle inside toward the journey of settling your soul down and seeking the gravity to pull you down to earth.
Trying to hide what is missing in your life for the sake of what is found.
Trying to tick some boxes and scratch some wishes from your list and keep the others with a question mark.

But for how long?
For how long can we hide and for how long can we live within this inner struggle?
For how long can we hide what we want for the sake of what we have, knowing that it was once our choice to agree on a certain life and knowing that any new decision to change or demand what is missing will jeopardize all other choices we made before?